# 故園畫憶

庚寅中秋
韓磬陸題

《故园画忆系列》编委会

**名誉主任**：韩启德

**主　　任**：邵　鸿

**委　　员**：（按姓氏笔画为序）

　　　　　　万　捷　　　王秋桂　　　方李莉　　　叶培贵

　　　　　　刘魁立　　　况　晗　　　严绍璗　　　吴为山

　　　　　　邵　鸿　　　范贻光　　　范　芳　　　孟　白

　　　　　　岳庆平　　　郑培凯　　　唐晓峰　　　曹兵武

故园画忆系列
Memory of the Old
Home in Sketches

# 滇东北印迹
Impression of Northeast Yunnan

宋　威　绘画　撰文
Sketches & Notes by Song Wei

学苑出版社
Academy Press

# 图书在版编目（CIP）数据

滇东北印迹 / 宋威绘画撰文. — 北京：学苑出版社，2020.10
（故园画忆系列）
ISBN 978-7-5077-6049-1

Ⅰ.①滇… Ⅱ.①宋… Ⅲ.①版画—作品集—中国—现代②云南—概况
Ⅳ.①J227②K927.4

中国版本图书馆CIP数据核字（2020）第200137号

| | |
|---|---|
| 出 版 人： | 孟　白 |
| 责任编辑： | 周　鼎　康　妮 |
| 出版发行： | 学苑出版社 |
| 社　　址： | 北京市丰台区南方庄2号院1号楼 |
| 邮政编码： | 100079 |
| 网　　址： | www.book001.com |
| 电子信箱： | xueyuanpress@163.com |
| 联系电话： | 010-67601101（营销部）、010-67603091（总编室） |
| 印 刷 厂： | 河北赛文印刷有限公司 |
| 开本尺寸： | 889×1194　1/24 |
| 印　　张： | 5 |
| 字　　数： | 120千字 |
| 图　　幅： | 99幅 |
| 版　　次： | 2020年10月第1版 |
| 印　　次： | 2020年10月第1次印刷 |
| 定　　价： | 45.00元 |

# 目录

序　非物质文化遗产与插画艺术　　　　李小明

**曲靖市**

| | |
|---|---|
| 油菜花海 | 3 |
| 九龙瀑布群风景区 | 4 |
| 白水塘 | 5 |
| 彩色沙林风景区 | 6 |
| 英武山生态旅游风景区 | 7 |
| 凤凰谷旅游风景区 | 8 |
| 沾益天坑 | 9 |
| 珠江源风景区 | 10 |
| 沾益彩云洞 | 11 |
| 海峰湿地 | 12 |
| 马龙野花沟 | 13 |
| 香炉山 | 14 |
| 十八连山国家森林公园 | 15 |
| 古敢水族乡 | 16 |
| 麒麟公园 | 17 |
| 南城门楼 | 18 |
| 靖宁宝塔 | 19 |
| 麒麟仙子雕塑 | 20 |
| 阿诗玛雕像 | 21 |
| "彩云之南·滴水三江"雕塑 | 22 |
| 三江女神雕塑 | 23 |
| 诸葛亮与孟获浮雕 | 24 |
| 爨宝子碑 | 25 |
| 会泽古城 | 26 |
| 会泽古城·会泽会馆 | 27 |
| 会泽文昌宫 | 28 |
| 大海乡石板房 | 29 |
| 布依族吊脚楼 | 30 |
| 雍家古民居 | 31 |
| 浦在廷故居 | 32 |
| 潦浒村土陶工艺 | 33 |
| 老厂酿酒 | 34 |
| 布依族 | 35 |
| 彝族大三弦舞 | 36 |
| 小蒲笋 | 37 |
| 高良乡纳平山村苗族蜡染·上蜡 | 38 |
| 高良乡纳平山村苗族蜡染·蜡染刀 | 39 |
| 五龙壮乡·节日 | 40 |
| 黑尔壮族服饰 | 41 |

| | |
|---|---|
| 彝族火草衬 | 42 |
| 彝族火把节 | 43 |
| 泡缸酒 | 44 |
| 擀毡 | 45 |
| 彝族服饰 | 46 |
| 古敢水族吞口舞 | 47 |
| 吞口 | 48 |
| 安迪村傣族跳脚舞 | 49 |
| 龙场猫耳斗 | 50 |
| 宣威火腿 | 51 |
| 倘塘黄豆腐 | 52 |

**昭通市**

| | |
|---|---|
| 大山包 | 55 |
| 大药山 | 56 |
| 赖石山 | 57 |
| 黄连河瀑布 | 58 |
| 大雪山原始森林 | 59 |
| 天台山溶洞 | 60 |
| 豆沙关 | 61 |
| 昭通古城 | 62 |
| 昭通古城·过街楼 | 63 |
| 昭通古城·昭通镇署衙门 | 64 |
| 昭通古城·八角亭 | 65 |
| 昭通古城·姜亮夫雕像 | 66 |

| | |
|---|---|
| 昭通古城·辕门口钟楼 | 67 |
| 大龙洞道观 | 68 |
| 清官亭 | 69 |
| 元宝山公园 | 70 |
| 望海公园 | 71 |
| 望海公园·恩波楼 | 72 |
| 望海公园·望海阁 | 73 |
| 老孔雀雕塑 | 74 |
| 罗炳辉将军像 | 75 |
| 昭通市博物馆 | 76 |
| 孟孝琚碑 | 77 |
| 拖姑清真寺·正殿 | 78 |
| 拖姑清真寺·唤醒楼 | 79 |
| 崇文阁 | 80 |
| 安氏土司墓 | 81 |
| 曾泽生将军故居 | 82 |
| 牛街古镇 | 83 |
| 罗炳辉将军故居 | 84 |
| 夫人坝 | 85 |
| 扎西会议纪念馆 | 86 |
| 扎西红军烈士陵园 | 87 |
| 水富港 | 88 |
| 向家坝水电站 | 89 |
| 昭通端公戏 | 90 |
| 昭通端公戏·面具 | 91 |

| | | | |
|---|---|---|---|
| 四筒鼓舞 | 92 | 小碗红糖 | 98 |
| 四筒鼓舞·四筒鼓 | 93 | 僰人悬棺 | 99 |
| 小寨樱桃 | 94 | 马楠苗族芦笙舞 | 100 |
| 回族刺绣 | 95 | 伍寨乡彝族月琴 | 101 |
| 梭山竹编 | 96 | 手工皮棉纸 | 102 |
| 炉房斑铜制作 | 97 | 芦笙制作 | 103 |

# Contents

Intangible Cultural Heritage and Illustration Art    Li Xiaoming

## Qujing City

| | |
|---|---|
| "Sea of Rape Flowers (Rape Flower Field)" | 3 |
| Scenic Zone of Jiulong Waterfalls | 4 |
| Baishui Pond | 5 |
| Scenic Zone of Colorful Sand Forest | 6 |
| Yingwu Mountain Eco-tourism Scenic Zone | 7 |
| Scenic Zone of Phoenix Valley | 8 |
| Zhanyi Sinkhole | 9 |
| Scenic Zone of Pearl River Source | 10 |
| Zhanyi Caiyun Cave | 11 |
| Haifeng Wetland | 12 |
| Wildflower Ditch | 13 |
| Censer Mountain | 14 |
| Shibalian Mountain National Forest Park | 15 |
| The Shui Township in Gugan | 16 |
| Kylin Park | 17 |
| South City Gate Tower | 18 |
| Jingning Pagoda | 19 |
| Sculpture of the Kylin Fairy | 20 |
| Ashimar Sculpture | 21 |
| Sculpture of "the South of Colorful Clouds, the Dripping of Sanjiang River" | 22 |
| Sculpture of the Sanjiang Goddess | 23 |
| Zhuge Liang and Menghuo Relievo | 24 |
| Cuan Baozi Stele | 25 |
| Huize Ancient City | 26 |
| Huize Ancient City · Huize Guild Hall | 27 |
| Huize Wenchang Palace | 28 |
| Slate House in Dahai Township | 29 |
| Stilted House of the Bouyei People | 30 |
| Yongjia Ancient Dwelling | 31 |
| Pu Zaiting's Former Residence | 32 |
| Earthenware Craft of Liaohu Village | 33 |
| Brewery of Laochang | 34 |
| The Bouyei Nationality | 35 |
| The Da Sanxian Dance of the Yi People | 36 |
| Small Puluo | 37 |
| Batik of the Miao People in Napingshan Village, Gaoliang Township · Waxing | 38 |
| Batik of the Miao in Napingshan Village, Gaoliang Township · Batik Knife | 39 |
| Wulong Zhuang Township · Festival | 40 |
| Costumes of the Zhuang in Heier | 41 |
| Fire-weed Jacket of the Yi People | 42 |

| | |
|---|---|
| Malong County · the Torch Festival of the Yi Nationality | 43 |
| Rice Wine fermented in the Jar | 44 |
| Making Felt | 45 |
| Costumes of the Yi People | 46 |
| The Tunkou Dance of the Shui Nationality in Gugan Township | 47 |
| Tunkou | 48 |
| Tiaojiao Dance of the Dai Nationality in Andi Village | 49 |
| Maoer Dou in Longchang County | 50 |
| Xuanwei Ham | 51 |
| Bean Curd of Tangtang Town | 52 |

### Zhaotong City

| | |
|---|---|
| Dashanbao | 55 |
| Dayao Mountain | 56 |
| Laishi Mountain | 57 |
| Huanglianhe Waterfall | 58 |
| Primitive Forest in Snow Mountain | 59 |
| The Karst Cave of Tiantai Mountain | 60 |
| Doushaguan Pass | 61 |
| Zhaotong Ancient City | 62 |
| Zhaotong Ancient City · Street-across Building | 63 |
| Zhaotong Ancient City · Yamen (government office) of Zhaotong Town | 64 |
| Zhaotong Ancient City · Bajiao (Octagonal) Pavilion | 65 |
| Zhaotong Ancient City · Jiang Liangfu Sculpture | 66 |
| Zhaotong Ancient City · Yuanmenkou Bell Tower | 67 |
| Taoist Temple in Dalong Cave | 68 |
| Qingguan (Honest and Upright Official) Pavilion | 69 |
| Yuanbaoshan Park | 70 |
| Wanghai (sea-viewing) Park | 71 |
| Wanghai Park · Enbo Tower | 72 |
| Wanghai Park · Wanghai Pavilion | 73 |
| Old Peacock Sculpture | 74 |
| Sculpture of General Luo Binghui | 75 |
| Zhaotong Museum | 76 |
| Meng Xiaoju Stele | 77 |
| Tuogu Mosque · Main Hall | 78 |
| Tuogu Mosque · Wakening Tower | 79 |
| Chongwen Pavilion | 80 |
| Chieftain Cemetery of the An | 81 |
| General Zeng Zesheng's Former Residence | 82 |
| Niujie Ancient Town | 83 |
| General Luo Binghui's Former Residence | 84 |
| Furen (lady) Dam | 85 |
| Memorial Hall of Zhaxi Meeting | 86 |
| Red Army Martyr Cemetery in Zhaxi Town | 87 |
| Shuifu Port | 88 |
| Xiangjiaba Hydropower Station | 89 |
| Duangong Opera in Zhaotong | 90 |
| Duangong Opera in Zhaotong · Mask | 91 |
| Si-tong Drum Dance | 92 |
| Si-tong Drum Dance · Si-tong Drum | 93 |
| Xiaozhai Cherry | 94 |
| Embroidery of the Hui Nationality | 95 |

| | |
|---|---|
| Suoshan Bamboo Weaving | 96 |
| Variegated Copperware Manufacturing in Lufang Township | 97 |
| Brown Sugar Contained by Small Bowl | 98 |
| Boren Suspending Coffin | 99 |
| Lusheng Dance of the Miao Nationality in Ma'nan | 100 |
| Yueqin of the Yi Nationality in Wuzhai Township | 101 |
| Handmade Lint Paper | 102 |
| Lusheng Manufacturing | 103 |

# 序
# 非物质文化遗产与插画艺术

插画是以画家描绘的图像来传播知识和人文故事的画种，因为多出现在出版物的文字中间，故称为插画或插图。与人们熟悉的中国画、油画、版画、水彩画等以画材工具命名的方式不同，插画作为一个画种却是从功能的角度来命名的。这一方面是由于插画在文化史上源远流长，已有上千年历史；另外则是社会发展到了信息社会却又进了读图时代，线上线下各种形式风格的插画成品蜂拥而来，冲击着人们的视觉世界，改变着人们观看和阅读的习惯。以插画为主、配以简明文字的绘本成了传播知识信息的重要途径，也是政府机构推动非物质文化遗产保护政策的有力工具。

云南地处祖国西南边陲，是多民族共同繁衍生长的民族文化宝库。昭通、曲靖地区又是连接中原汉文化与东南亚各民族文化的过渡地带，生活在当地的各族人民在生产与生活习惯上有着过渡地带互相渗透、兼容并蓄的特点。曲靖、昭通也是云南开通滇越线之前自古通往中原、内地的主要水陆交通要道，沿途物产丰富、文化昌明，有东川等全国主要铜矿产地。商贾不绝于途，可以说是云南的早开发地带。后因滇黔、滇桂、成昆线开通，铁路、海路取代了以畜力为主的川滇古道。失去运输通道、人流物流的支撑，昭通等地逐渐回落到农耕经济，矿产资源结束商业周期，整个区域又隐退至经济版图的边缘，文化昌明也随之隐身于历史大幕的背后。虽然也有"文化现象"突现的个例如流星划过夜空，使人遥想曾经的繁荣，令人不胜感慨，因此更加期待今人的努力能创造更新更美的画卷以再续往昔的胜景。

非物质文化遗产保护的是人类的情感与记忆。对同样属于文化遗产的他国民族文化，人们持理解、欣赏的距离感，对本国的民族文化则更加亲近与认同。这源于文化基因与情感倚托，这种感情认知来自长期共同生活于相同的社会人文环境的教育与熏陶。宋威完成的这套作品正是这样的文化建设，通过图文并茂的插画形象地展示了曲靖、昭通两地的非遗项目，构筑了人们共同的文化记忆，增进了各民族的团结。如果能进一步提高读者对非遗保护事业的了解与支持，那正是本书创作出版的初心所在。作者宋威是位画家和教师，从附中到硕士毕业，经历吉林艺术学院、西安美术学院、深圳大学、云南艺术学院的专业训练与教学实践的磨炼。他埋头版画的创作与研究，尤其是对插画这一古老而又新颖画种的研究。作为专业教师，他一直主理着云艺插画专业的本科教学工作，教学成绩斐然。希望宋威再接再厉、坚持不懈、沉毅努力，为版画和插画事业做出更亮眼的贡献。

是为序。

李小明

中国美术家协会会员

云南艺术学院原副院长

云南省美术家协会原副主席

云南艺术学院教授、硕士研究生导师

# Intangible Cultural Heritage and Illustration Art

Yunnan, located in the southwest border of China, is a treasure house of national culture nurtured by multiple ethnic groups. As Zhaotong and Qujing are the transition zones connecting the Han culture in the central plains with the cultures of various ethnic groups in Southeast Asia, people living there are characterized with all-embracing inclusiveness in terms of production and life style.

Qujing and Zhaotong also serve as the main water and land transport routes leading to the central plains before the launch of the Yunnan-Vietnam Railway in Yunnan. Areas along the way abound in natural resources and thriving culture with merchants coming and going. So it's fair to say that Qujing and Zhaotong are among the earliest developed zones in Yunnan. Later, as railway and sea transport replaced the animal transport-driven Sichuan-Yunnan Ancient Road, Zhaotong and other places lost the support of transport corridors, stream of people and logistics, and gradually fell back to the agricultural economy. Similarly, the whole region took a back seat to the edge of the economic landscape, followed by the hiding of the flourishing culture behind the curtain of history.

Some "cultural phenomena" popping up, though, reminds people of the once-thriving past. People of today therefore are more expected to strive to continue the splendid past.

Intangible cultural heritage is supposed to protect human emotions and memories. People have more cultural affinity toward their mother country's culture compared with that of others. This emotion-related cognition is rooted in cultural genes and emotional sustenance, and is originated from the education and edification of living together in the same social environment for a long time.

This set of work authored by Song Wei exactly demonstrates such cultural significance. With the help of text-assisted illustrations, this work vividly displays the intangible programs in Qujing and Zhaotong, building people's common cultural memory and united ties among various nationalities.

The original aspiration behind this work is to win readers' understanding of and support for the protection of intangible cultural heritage. The author of this work, Song Wei, is a painter and teacher who has been cultivated by professional training and teaching practices in Jilin University of the Arts, Xi'an Academy of Fine Arts, Shenzhen University and Yunnan Arts University.

He immersed himself in the creation and research of print, especially the study of illustration, a painting with a mixture of antiquity and novelty. As a professional teacher, he has been in charge of undergraduate teaching and has made outstanding achievements in this regard. I hope Song Wei can contribute greater highlights to the undertaking of print and illustration with persistence and unremitting efforts.

This serves the preface.

Li Xiaoming

Member of China Artists Association

Former Vice President, Yunnan Arts University

Former Vice Chairman, Chinese Artists Association of Yunnan Province

Professor and Graduate Supervisor, Yunnan Arts University

## 曲靖市
Qujing City

{油菜花海}

位于曲靖市罗平县。罗平县是我国的油菜生产基地和蜜蜂春繁、蜂产品加工基地。每年2、3月份，油菜花在罗平坝子竞相争放，放眼望去，是一片一望无际的金黄。

## "Sea of Rape Flowers (Rape Flower Field)"

It is located in Luoping County, Qujing City. Luoping County is China's base of rape flowers production. Every year in February and March, rape flowers in Luoping Bazi (Dam) are in full blossom.

### 九龙瀑布群风景区

　　位于曲靖市罗平县城北 22 千米处。由于特殊的地质构造和水流的千年侵蚀，形成了十级高低宽窄不等、形态各异的瀑布群。其中最大一级宽 112 米，高 56 米，气势恢宏，号称"九龙第一瀑"。九龙瀑布群有"九龙十瀑，南国一绝"的美誉。

### Scenic Zone of Jiulong Waterfalls

It is located 22 kilometers away from the north of Luoping County, Qujing City. Waterfalls with various forms took shape under the specific geographic construction and thousand-year erosion of flowing water, in which the largest one is 112 meters wide and 56 meters high.

### 白水塘

  位于曲靖市陆良县南盘江和杜公河之间。白水塘总面积1.6平方千米,深2米,南北长,东西窄,水源主要来自雨水。因盛夏水域广大、白浪滔天,故得名白水塘。

## Baishui Pond

It is located between the Nanpan River and the Dugong River in Luliang County, Qujing City. With a total area of 1.6 square kilometers and a depth of 2 meters, Baishui Pond is long from north to south and narrow from east to west, with rainfalls as its main source of water.

### 彩色沙林风景区

位于曲靖市陆良县。该沙林由风化剥蚀而成，因季节、气候、日照及观赏角度的不同，会产生绚丽多变的色彩，故得名彩色沙林。占地 25 平方千米，保护区面积 52.8 平方千米。是云南省著名的地质旅游景观。

**Scenic Zone of Colorful Sand Forest**

Located in Luliang County, Qujing City, this sand forest is formed under the impact of weathering and denudation. The forest presents different, gorgeous and changeable colors in different seasons, climates, under sunlight or when viewed from different perspectives. Hence, it was given the name "Colorful Sand Forest".

{ 英武山生态旅游风景区 }

  俗称菌子山，位于曲靖市师宗县东南部，是师宗县境内最高的山脉，海拔 2409.7 米。英武山风景区气候温和湿润，森林覆盖面积超过 90%，总面积约 30 平方千米，景区内有丰富的动、植物资源。

## Yingwu Mountain Eco-tourism Scenic Zone

Yingwu Mountain is commonly known as Junzi Mountain, lying in the southeastern part of Shizong County, Qujing City. It is the highest mountain in Shizong County, with an altitude of 2409.7 meters.

### 凤凰谷旅游风景区

位于曲靖市师宗县五龙壮族乡，平均海拔 1200 米，景区面积 180 平方千米。因洞中有形似凤凰的钟乳石，古称岩凤峡，传说是凤凰涅槃的圣地。为世界第一高洞，溶洞垂直高度 218 米。

## Scenic Zone of Phoenix Valley

It is located in Wulong Zhuang Autonomous Township, Shizong County, Qujing City, at an average elevation of 1,200 meters above sea level and with a scenic area of 180 square kilometers. Phoenix Valley was named as Yanfeng Gorge in ancient times because the stalactites in the cave are shaped like phoenix.

### 沾益天坑

位于曲靖市沾益区大坡海峰湿地自然保护区。是云南最大的自然天坑，天坑四周均为90度悬崖峭壁，底部有喀斯特地貌深洞，坑内长有特殊的植物群落。

### Zhanyi Sinkhole

Located in Haifeng Wetland Nature Reserve, Dafeng Township, Zhanyi District, Qujing City, Zhanyi Tiankeng serves as Yunnan's largest nature Sinkhole of its kind. It is surrounded by 90-degree cliffs, with deep karst caves at the bottom.

### 珠江源风景区

　　位于曲靖市沾益区境内马雄山麓。景区面积 12.5 平方千米，主峰海拔 2444 米。景区内有马樱花、伏地松、天下第一罗盘、天下第一棋盘、珠江源石牌坊、珠源第一瀑、霞客草堂、珠江禅寺等景观。

### Scenic Zone of Pearl River Source

It is situated at the foot of Maxiong Mountain in Zhanyi District, Qujing City. The scenic spot covers 12.5 square kilometers and the main peak therein is 2,444 meters above the sea level.

沾益彩云洞

　　位于曲靖市沾益区盘江镇。彩云洞为一天然暗洞，洞长约 3 千米，洞体宽敞，由钟乳石自然分隔成 6 个不同的景区。其洞内的岩石有红、白、黄、黑、赫、紫等多种色彩。

## Zhanyi Caiyun Cave

Located in Panjiang Town, Zhanyi District, Qujing City, Caiyun Cave is a natural dark cave with a length of some 3 kilometers and is divided by stalactites into 6 different scenic spots.

海峰湿地

　　位于曲靖市沾益区。海峰湿地有"云南小桂林"之誉，是云南省海拔最低、纬度最低的湿地。景区面积6.67平方千米，散落着大大小小的石峰、石林、溶洞、天坑以及大面积的沼泽地，并栖息有黑颈鹤、黑鹳、白鹤等多种国家一级保护动物。

## Haifeng Wetland

Located in Zhanyi District, Qujing City, it serves as a wetland at the lowest altitude and latitude in Yunnan Province. The scenic spot covers an area of 6.67 square kilometers.

### 马龙野花沟

　　位于曲靖市马龙县西南部马鸣乡境内，深藏于马鸣乡80平方千米深的原始森林中，为典型的原始河谷风貌。野花沟延绵10千米，一年四季繁花盛开、流水潺潺。

### Wildflower Ditch

Located in Maming Township, the southwestern part of Malong County, Qujing City, the wildflower ditch is hidden in the 80-square kilometer primitive forest. It spreads 10 kilometers, with flowers blossoming the whole year.

香炉山

　　位于曲靖市马龙县城西 40 千米的马鞍山北面。香炉山海拔 2010.8 米，山岩陡峭，因远视型同香炉而得名。据《续修马龙县志》记载，历史上曾有著名的"马龙八景"，香炉山的"香炉倚空"为八景之一。

## Censer Mountain

It is located in the north side of Ma'an Mountain, 40 kilometers from the western part of Malong County, Quqing County. Censer Mountain stands 2010.8 meters above the sea level with steep rocks and stones and is named so as it looks like a censer from afar.

### 十八连山国家森林公园

　　位于曲靖市富源县,地处滇黔交界的黄泥河和块泽河分水岭的南延部分,景区面积10平方千米。景区内有棋盘星、三棵桩滴水岩、燕子洞、模儿洞、仙人洞等景点。

### Shibalian Mountain National Forest Park

Located in Fuyuan County, Qujing City, it sits at the southern extension of watershed between Huangni River and Kuaize River, where Yunnan Province and Guizhou Province meet. Covering 10 square kilometers, this scenic area is home to spots such as Check-board Star and Xianrendong Cave.

{ 古敢水族乡 }

　　位于曲靖市富源县东南部的云贵交界处，是贵州省黔西南州进入富源、盘县的必经之路，有"滇黔锁钥"之称。全乡总面积 82.6 平方千米，境内居住着汉、水、彝、苗、白、回、布依和蒙古 8 个民族。

## The Shui Township in Gugan

It is located in the intersection of Yunnan Province and Guizhou Province, the southeastern part of Fuyuan County, Qujing City. This township, which covers an area of 82.6 square kilometers, is home to eight ethnic groups, namely Han, Shui, Yi, Miao, Bai, Hui, Bouyei and Mongolian.

**麒麟公园**

  位于曲靖市麒麟区。建于 1983 年，占地 10 万平方米。公园正门高大雄伟，气宇轩昂，富有民族特色。园内亭、台、楼、榭等建筑古色古香，布局精巧雅致，充满魅力。

## Kylin Park

Located in Qilin District, Qujing City, this park was established in 1983, covering an area of 100,000 square meters. The pavilions, terraces and other buildings therein present classic beauty and follow an elegant and delicate layout.

### 南城门楼

　　位于曲靖市麒麟区原南城门楼东150米之老城埂上，1997年7月1日竣工。城楼立高35米，其中城高20米，楼高15米。飞檐翘角宫殿式建筑，分为主楼和东西二楼，三、四楼四壁雕刻有"红楼梦"大型连环浮雕334幅。

### South City Gate Tower

Located on the ridge of the old city, 150 meters from the east of the former South City Gate Tower in Qilin District, Qujing City, it was completed on July 1st, 1997. This palace-style building, 35 meters high, is divided into the main tower, the east tower and the west tower.

{ 靖宁宝塔 }

位于曲靖市麒麟区城边的寥廓山顶，建于 2010 年。塔高 81.6 米，为楼阁式塔，仿明清古建筑风格，是在云南地区最高的一座仿古塔。

## Jingning Pagoda

Located at the top of Liaokuo Mountain on the edge of Qilin District, Qujing City, it was established in 2010. The pavilion-style pagoda is 81.6 meters high and was established imitating the style of ancient buildings in the Ming and Qing dynasties (1368–1911A.D.).

### 麒麟仙子雕塑

　　位于曲靖市麒麟区麒麟南路、麒麟北路、麒麟东路、麒麟西路和交通路南口五条道路交汇处。建于1982年。该雕塑为曲靖市地标性建筑，高3.8米，用高3.55米的基座托起。相传古时曲靖城大旱，一位美丽的仙女骑着一头麒麟临空而降，并洒下了一场大雨，曲靖因此获救。

### Sculpture of the Kylin Fairy

It is located in the intersection of five roads, namely Qilin South Road, Qilin North Road, Qilin East Road, Qilin West Road and south-junction of Jiaotong Road. Established in 1982, this 3.8-meter in height sculpture represents a landmark of Qujing City.

### 阿诗玛雕像

位于曲靖市麒麟区，建于1982年。雕塑由四川美术学院雕塑系教授冯宜贵创作，内容取材于撒尼人著名的叙事长诗——阿诗玛。高2.9米，长3.2米，由高9.4米的人工石峰托起，雕塑手法粗犷有力，表现了一种力度强劲的刚强雄健形象。

### Ashimar Sculpture

Located in Qilin District, Qujin City, this sculpture, 2.9 meters high and 3.2 meters long, was established in 1982. It is originated from the renowned narrative poem Ashimar created by Sani people.

## "彩云之南·滴水三江"雕塑

　　位于曲靖市麒麟区大花桥铁路公路交界处街心花园的中央环岛处。整体造型为三根不锈钢柱子支撑着上空与柱子相连的七彩祥云。高 28 米，彩云部分长 20 米、宽 10 米。彩云象征着祥瑞和谐，三根不锈钢水柱代表曲靖珠江源头"一水注三江"的独特地理风貌。

**Sculpture of "the South of Colorful Clouds, the Dripping of Sanjiang River"**
It is located in the intersection of Dahuaqiao railway and highway thereof in Qilin District, Qujing City. The general structure of this 28-meter high sculpture is that three columns made of stainless steel are propping the above-connected seven-color auspicious clouds.

## 三江女神雕塑

位于曲靖市麒麟区。建于2001年，由雕塑家叶毓山设计制作完成。高8.3米，重180吨，汉白玉石制。雕塑由三位女神构成，两个女神面向东方，寓示两条江水向东流后汇入珠江；一个女神面向西方，寓示牛栏江水向西流入长江。其上的山川、谷物、麦穗图案象征着曲靖丰富的物产资源。

## Sculpture of the Sanjiang Goddess

Located in Qilin District, Qujing City, it was established in 2001 designed by sculptor Ye Yushan. The white marble-made sculpture, as high as 8.3 meters, is constituted by three goddesses with carved patterns such as mountains, rivers, grains and ears of wheat on it, symbolizing the abundant natural resources in Qujing.

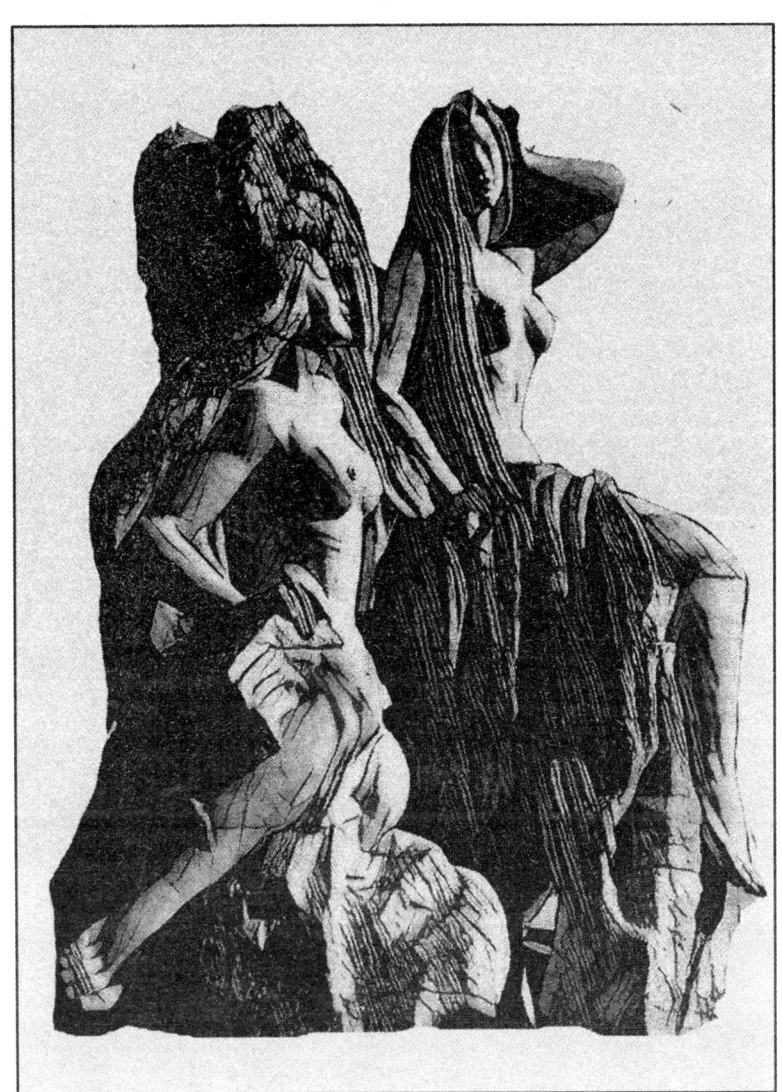

### 诸葛亮与孟获浮雕

　　位于曲靖市麒麟区白石江畔。长60米，高4米，由黑色大理石雕刻而成，总面积240平方米。浮雕再现了1000多年前的三国时期，诸葛亮南征七擒七纵云南少数民族头领孟获之后，与孟获举杯言和的动人场面。

### Zhuge Liang and Menghuo Relievo

It is located in the bank of Baishi River in Qilin District, Qujing City. 60 meters long and 4 meters high, this relievo is made of black marble, re-displaying the scene where Zhuge Liang and Menghuo, the leader of ethnic minorities in Yunnan, proposed the toast to bury the hatchet.

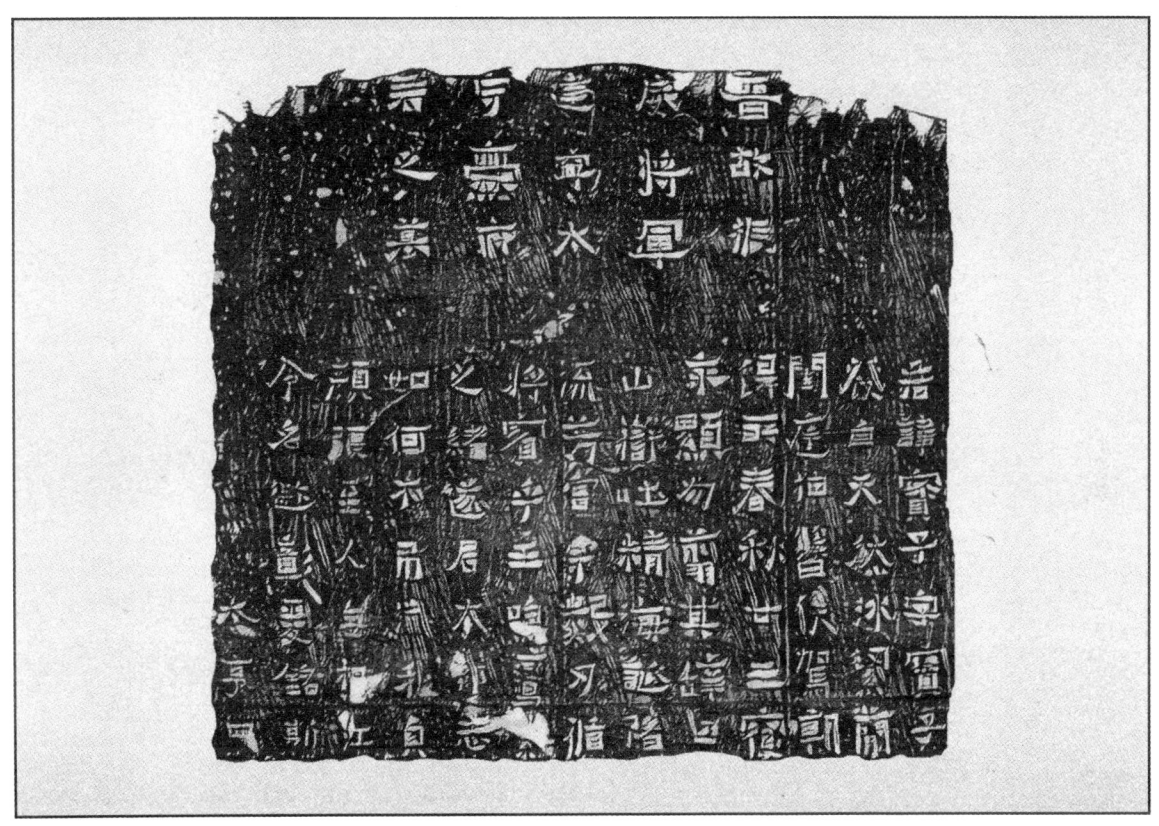

### 爨宝子碑

位于曲靖市麒麟区曲靖一中内。爨宝子碑全称"晋故振威将军建宁太守爨府君墓"碑，清乾隆四十三年（1778年）出土于曲靖市区南扬旗田。碑为长方形，额半圆形，高1.83米，宽0.68米，厚0.21米。碑文字体是从隶书向楷书过渡文体，结构古朴，古气盎然。

### Cuan Baozi Stele

It is located in Qujing No.1 Middle School of Qilin District, Qujing City. This rectangle-shaped stele was unearthed in Qujing urban district in 1778 (the 43rd year during the reign of Emperor Qianlong in the Qing Dynasty), and is 1.83 meters high, 0.68 meters wide and 0.21 meters thick.

会泽古城

　　位于曲靖市会泽县。建于清雍正九年（1731年），由时任东川知府崔乃镛主持建造。城区范围北到义通河、南至钟屏街、东到翠屏街、西至京运大街，面积约0.95平方千米。十字街是古城的中心，古城内会馆林立、寺庙众多。

## Huize Ancient City

It is located in Huize County, Qujing City. It was built in 1731 (the 9th year during the reign of Emperor Yongzheng in the Qing Dynasty) under the direction of Cui Naiyong, Dongchuan county magistrate at that time. Covering an area of 0.95 square kilometers, this ancient city boasts many guild halls and temples.

**会泽古城·会泽会馆**

位于会泽古城内。会泽会馆是古代各省和府在会泽建盖的会馆的统称，以八大会馆为代表。该建筑群落堪称"清代古建博物馆"，是研究清代建筑艺术、铜商文化的珍贵实物资料。

## Huize Ancient City · Huize Guild Hall

Located in Huize Ancient City, Huize guild hall serves as the generic term of guild halls built by provinces and prefectures at all levels in Huize in ancient times, which is represented by Eight Great Guild Halls. These halls are precious physical materials for study on architecture art of the Qing Dynasty (1636–1911A.D.).

## 会泽文昌宫

位于曲靖市会泽县城南的金钟山巅，系清雍正五年（1727年）东川知府黄士杰和赵淳主持兴建，占地8000平方米。文昌宫主体建筑有牌楼、魁阁、戏台、对厅、大殿等，正殿前檐正中挂有"天上文衡"匾额，殿内有文昌帝君和两童子塑像。

## Huize Wenchang Palace

Sitting at Huize County, Qujing City, the palace was built in 1727 (the 5th year during the reign of Emperor Yongzheng in the Qing Dynasty) under the direction of Huang Shijie (the Dongchuan country magistrate at that time) and Zhao Chun. It covers an area of 8,000 square meters and the main architectures therein are memorial archways, drama stages and main halls.

### 大海乡石板房

　　位于曲靖市会泽县大海乡。大海乡有滇东北"小西藏"之称，海拔高、气温低，因传统汉族瓦屋面住房不能适应当地的自然环境，石板房由此而生。石板房为土木石混合建筑，依山而建，一般高 4.2 米，长 11 米，宽 5.2 米。四室一厅，两间耳房用作住宿，中间堂屋用来招待客人。

### Slate House in Dahai Township

Located in Dahai Township, Huize County, Qujing City, the slate house is a mixed building established with earth, wood and stone, standing against the mountain. It is 4.2 meters high, 11 meters long with 4 rooms and one hall. Two side rooms thereof are used for accommodation and the central room for hospitality.

{ 布依族吊脚楼 }

    位于曲靖市罗平县鲁布革乡。布依族吊脚楼的建筑形态，源于其所处的自然环境。为了抵御外来侵害，布依族利用现成的大树作架，铺上野竹树条，在顶上搭架子盖顶棚，修筑起空中楼阁，后逐渐发展成现在的吊脚楼建筑。

## Stilted House of the Bouyei People

It is located in Buge Township, Luoping County, Qujing City. In order to defend against external invasions, the Bouyei people used ready-made big trees as framework to build house in the air which gradually evolved into today's stilted houses.

### 雍家古民居

　　位于曲靖市陆良县芳华镇。雍家古村是家族式聚落古民居建筑群。古村坐东向西，在南、北、西三面各设有一道大门，进入大门后形成网状式阁巷，通往每户人家。各户均为四合院汉民居建筑，四合院内相互连接贯通，宛如一个巨大的迷宫。

### Yongjia Ancient Dwelling

Situated in Fanghua Town, Luliang County, Qujing City, the ancient dwelling sits facing the west. There is a gate in the south, north and west side respectively, forming grid-style alleys leading to each household therein.

浦在廷故居

　　位于宣威市西城下街 27 号。浦在廷（1871 年~1950 年），宣威榕城镇人，邓小平夫人卓琳的父亲，云南宣威火腿罐头的创始人。故居建于民国初年，为一楼一底回廊式四合院，东西长 100 米，南北宽 15 米，占地 1500 平方米。该建筑系二进院式汉民居住宅，具有江南汉式民居的典型特征。

**Pu Zaiting's Former Residence**
It is located in No.27, Lower Xicheng Street, Xuanwei City, Qujing City. Pu Zaiting (1897–1950), a native of Rongcheng Town in Xuanwei, is the forefather of Xuanwei canned ham. The former residence, established in the early years of the Republic of China, is a corridor-style Siheyuan (quadrangle courtyard) with two stories. It is 100 meters long from west to east, 15 meters wide from north to south, covering 1,500 square meters.

### 潦浒村土陶工艺

　　曲靖市麒麟区越州镇潦浒村,是一座有千年制陶历史的古村镇,素有"土陶之乡"的美称。在潦浒南盘江东岸的贝丘遗址,发现有距今约 2700 多年的夹砂灰陶。潦浒陶瓷制作历史悠久,制陶方式较多,既有古代烧柴的龙窑、蒲萝窑,也有近代烧煤的隧道窑、辊道窑以及现代化的气窑和电窑,可谓是陶瓷生产的历史博物馆。

### Earthenware Craft of Liaohu Village

Liaohu Village in Yuezhou County, Qilin District, Qujing City enjoys the reputation of "the hometown of earthenware". Ceramics manufacturing in Liaohu embraces a long history. There are many manufacturing methods, including wood-burning longyao (dragon kiln) in ancient times, coal-burning suidaoyao (tunnel kiln) in modern time and today's modernized dianyao (electrical kiln).

### 老厂酿酒

　　罗平县苞谷酒，因产于虎山脚下的老厂村，故名老厂酒。老厂酒已有150多年的酿造历史。不加酒精的纯玉米发酵法、当地独特的高品质清泉水和铜锅酿造工艺，使老厂酒酒质醇厚、浓香扑鼻。

### Brewery of Laochang

Liquor produced in Laochang Village, Luoping County enjoys a history of more than 150 years. Fermentation of pure corn without adding alcohol, coupled with brewing technologies which uses locally unique and high-quality spring water and copper pan give mellow texture and robust scents to the wine.

### 布依族

罗平布依族占云南省布依族人口的80%，布依族有语言而无文字，服饰以蓝、黑、青三色为主。传统节日有农历"二月二"、"三月三"对歌节和"祭老人房"等。布依族的舞蹈很有特色，种类繁多，主要有"织布舞""伴嫁舞""狮子舞""龙舞""铜鼓舞"等。

### The Bouyei Nationality

The population of the Bouyei nationality in Luoping County accounts for 80% of the Bouyei people in Yunnan Province. The Bouyei people have their own language but no writing system, and their costumes are mainly in blue, black and cyan. They also celebrate several traditional festivals such as February 2 of lunar calendar, March 3 of lunar calendar (a festival for singing in antiphonal style) and the Village-God worship.

**彝族大三弦舞**

大三弦舞是彝族支系撒尼人的传统民间舞蹈。撒尼人每逢节庆日和一些农闲时候，都要跳大三弦舞。特别是火把节，人们燃起篝火、点上火把，围着篝火弹起"大三弦"载歌载舞。舞蹈始终保持跳跃状态，双臂左右摆动、按节拍击掌的同时，换脚跳三步，空中蹬两脚。整个舞蹈动作幅度较大、粗犷豪放，气氛热烈而欢快。

**The Da Sanxian Dance of the Yi People**

It is a traditional folk dance of the Sani people (a branch of the Yi nationality). Bouncing and jumping run through this dance. As the dancer shakes his or her arms from side to side and claps the hands following the beat, he or she jumps three steps while changing foot and makes two kicks in the air.

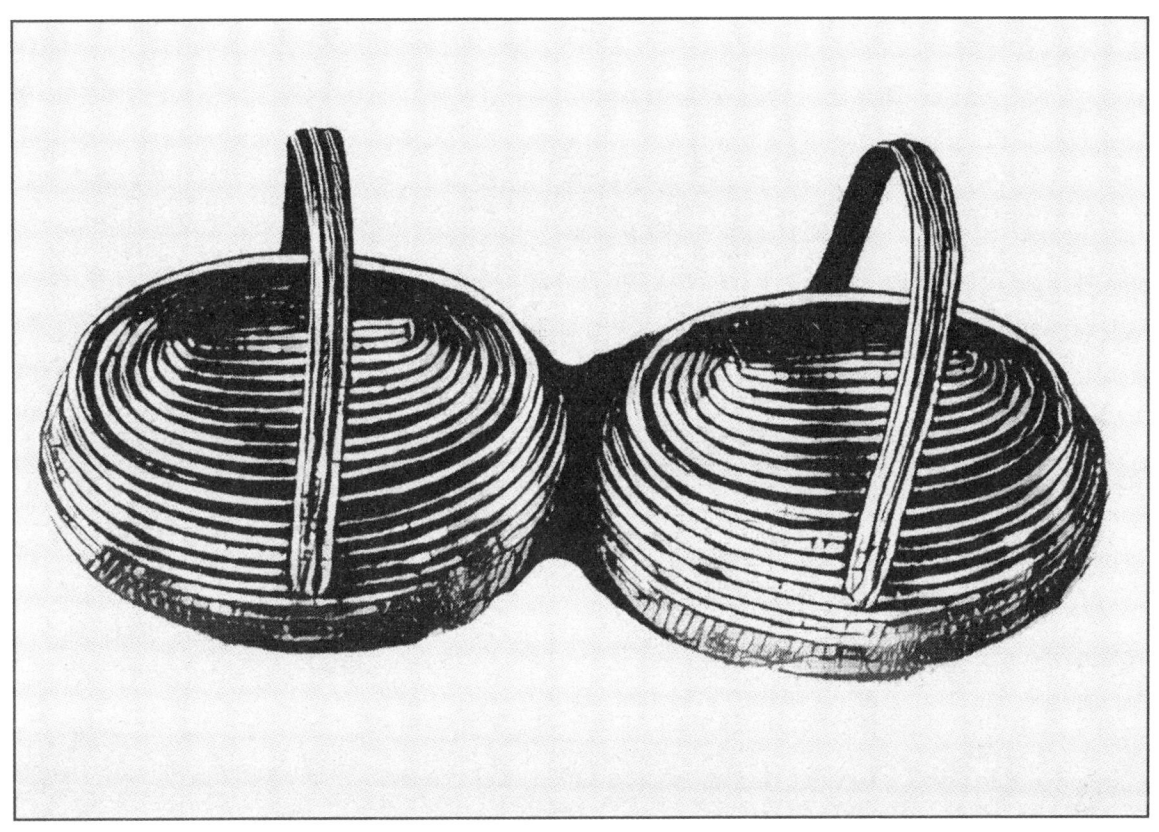

小蒲箩

陆良县小蒲箩的编织历史已有 300 多年,相传由浙江金华一位嫁到该村的女子传入。蒲箩可大可小,大的叫大蒲箩,可做草帽、锅盖等用;小的可做针线篮。

Small Puluo

It enjoys a weaving history of more than 300 years. Puluo could be big and small. The big one can be made straw hat and pan cover while the small one can made basket for containing needles and threads.

高良乡纳平山村苗族蜡染·上蜡

　　蜡染是苗族的一项传统手工艺，主要产品有衣、裤、裙、包头、腰带、绑腿、背包等。上蜡为蜡染的工序之一，主要作用是保持麻原料的原有色泽。蜡液对麻布形成保护层，不仅可以延长使用寿命，也可以增加美观性。

### Batik of the Miao People in Napingshan Village, Gaoliang Township · Waxing

Batik marks a traditional handicraft of the Miao nationality, waxing being one of the working procedures thereof. Waxing is to maintain the original color of the raw material hemp and at the same time form a protective layer for the hessian to ensure its prolonged life.

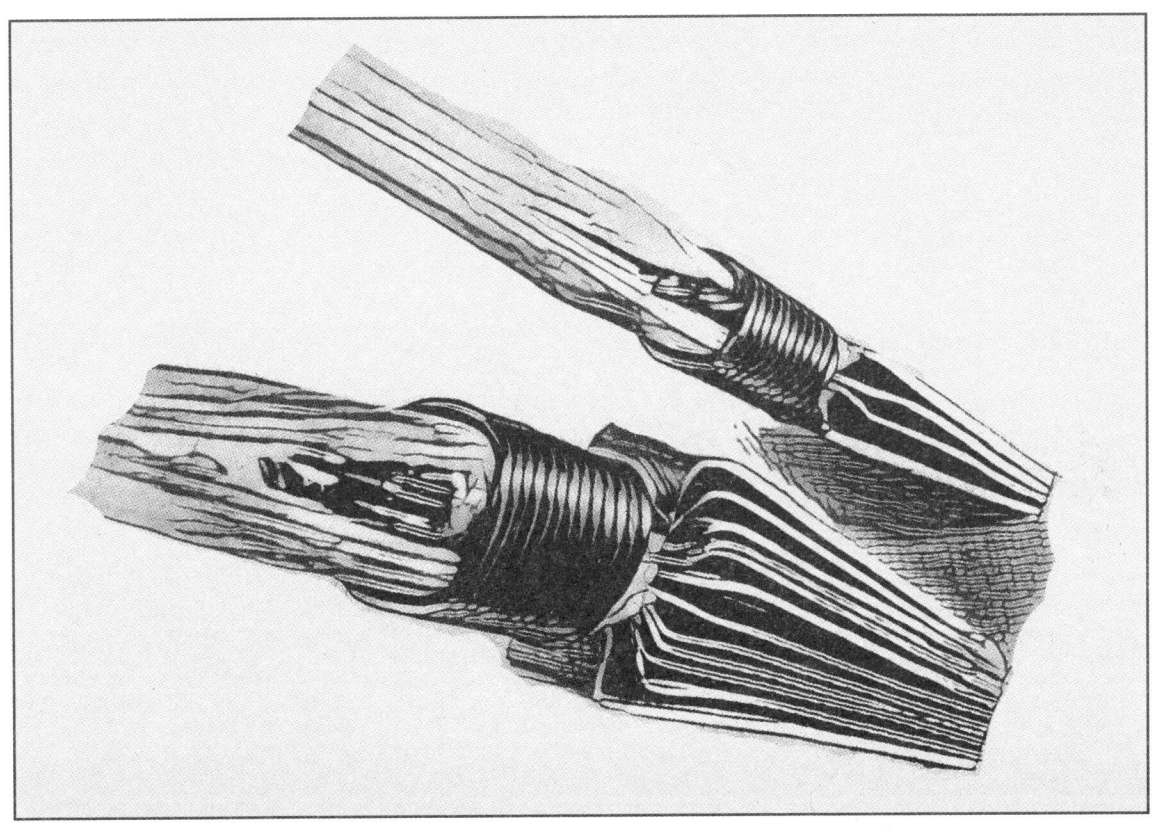

高良乡纳平山村苗族蜡染·蜡染刀

　　蜡染刀由几片扇形黄铜薄片等距绑在一起制成，铜片与铜片之间的缝隙使蘸蜡时可以保存更多的蜡液，方便给布面上蜡。

**Batik of the Miao in Napingshan Village, Gaoliang Township · Batik Knife**
Batik knife is made by equidistant bonding of several fan-shaped brass sheets. The gap between two brass sheets allows more melted wax to be preserved when the knife is dipped in wax.

### 五龙壮乡·节日

　　五龙，壮语的发音是"西纳"，意为风景美丽、田水富饶的鱼米之乡。五龙壮乡人热情好客，每年农历三月三日，是壮家人的节日，三天的时间里，有长廊壮宴、竹筏戏水、壮族小调、百米竹竿舞、狂欢泼水等众多活动举行。

### Wulong Zhuang Township · Festival

"Wulong" in the Zhuang language is pronounced as "Xi'na" which means an abundant place with beautiful scenery and fertile soil and water. Each March 3 of lunar calendar marks a special festival for the Zhuang people on which many activities such as dabbling on bamboo raft and water-sprinkling carnival are held.

### 黑尔壮族服饰

黑尔位于曲靖、文山、红河三市州交界处，为壮族村落，以黑尔糯米、糍粑、民族服饰而闻名。黑尔壮族服饰原料有自种棉花、丝线、银器等。将棉花制成布，进行印染，最后在布上缝制各种花纹图案，并加上各种银饰装点，十分有特色。

### Costumes of the Zhuang in Heier

Heier is a village of the Zhuang, which is located in the intersection where Qujing City, Wenshan City and Honghe Hani and Yi Autonomous Prefecture meet. The costumes of the Zhuang in Heier are very unique and their production steps are as follows: first, the cottons are made into cloths; second, the cloths are printed and dyed; finally, the cloths are embroiled with floral patterns and decorated with silver-made ornaments.

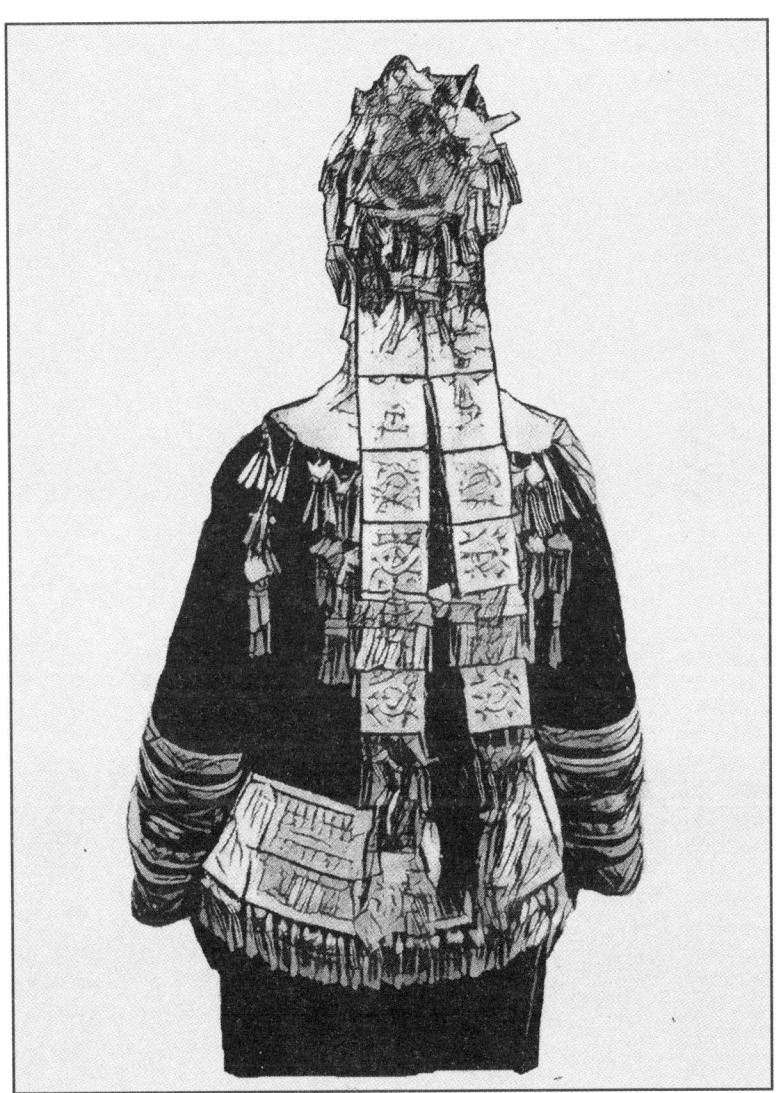

### 彝族火草褂

彝族是马龙县的土著民族,马龙县马鸣乡咨卡彝族村有制作火草褂的传统。火草褂由野火草叶子背面的白色绒状物纺织而成,工序繁复。制成的草褂色白微黄,穿着柔软,保温性能好,且十分耐穿。

### Fire-weed Jacket of the Yi People

It is a tradition of making fire-weed jackets in the Zika Yi Village, Maming Township, Malong County. Fire-weed jacket is woven from the white villi-form substance on the underside of wild fire-weed leaves. The already made jacket, white mixed with pale yellow, is very durable.

### 彝族火把节

　　火把节是彝族的传统盛大节日,在每年农历六月二十四日举行,时间一至三天不等。火把节源于对火与自然的崇拜,其目的是期望用火驱虫除害、保护庄稼生长。火把节是彝族历史文化的缩影,反映了彝族人民乐观向上的精神。

## Malong County · the Torch Festival of the Yi Nationality

The torch festival is a grand traditional festival of the Yi Nationality, which falls on every June 24 of lunar calendar and its duration varies from one to three days. This festival is derived from the worship of fire and the Nature, aiming at protecting the growth of crops from pests with the help of fire.

### 泡缸酒

泡缸酒是彝族特制的一种酒，早在三国时期，就已经用来祭祀、祈神，至今已有 1700 多年的历史。泡缸酒用大米发酵制成，状如米汤，味道清甜，口感绵长。

### Rice Wine fermented in the Jar

It is exclusively made by the Yi people, enjoying a history of over 1,700 years. This wine, made by rice fermentation, looks like rice soup and tastes fresh and sweet.

擀 毡

会泽县大桥乡的擀毡工艺有上百年的历史，擀毡在当地也叫"煮毡"，选用高原绵羊三月毛、六月毛和九月毛为主要原材料，经过打、铺、揉、画、染、洗、晒等多道工序手工制作而成。从色彩上看，可分为白毡、红毡、多色图毡等。

## Making Felt

The processes of making felt in Daqiao Township, Huize County have a history of some 100 years. Fleeces from plateau sheep in March, June and September are selected as main raw materials to make this felt by hand through several procedures.

### 彝族服饰

彝族服饰风格独特、工序繁杂，从纺线、浸染、织布、裁剪到刺绣，全部手工完成，尤以刺绣工艺最为精致。例如图中的围腰刺绣，非常精美。围腰即可用于装钱、副食品等，也可以在炒菜时防止油溅在身上。

### Costumes of the Yi People

The embroidery of costumes of the Yi people stands out as the most exquisite and elegant part, which can be demonstrated by the embroidery on the apron shown in the picture. The apron can not only be used as a container for money, non-staple food and other items, but also a shield to prevent oil from splashing on the body when cooking.

### 古敢水族吞口舞

富源县古敢乡是云南唯一的水族乡。吞口舞又名耍吞口，水语发音为"浪及根"，有神守护、妖邪勿近之意，是水族特有的民间传统舞蹈。舞蹈表演者大多为强壮的中青年男子，表演时手握吞口面具在胸，一边念咒吼叫，一边马步跳跃，动作刚劲有力，富于生机与活力。

### The Tunkou Dance of the Shui Nationality in Gugan Township

Gugan Township in Fuyuan County is the only locality of the Shui people in Yunnan. Tunkou dance represents a unique traditional folk dance of the Shui and the dancers are mainly able-bodied young and middle-aged men. When dancing, the dancers hold a tunkou mask on the chest. They also incant and shout while jumping with horse-riding steps.

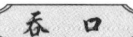

吞口

　　吞口为人头傩像，起源于图腾崇拜和原始巫教，是古代图腾文化与巫文化相结合的产物。吞口以白扬、柳木为主要原材料进行雕刻。木材大小没有固定模式，可大可小、可圆可方。雕刻后用沙子打磨光滑，最后涂上油漆。

**Tunkou**

Tunkou is a Nuo statue with human head, serving as the fruit of the integration of totem culture and Wu (witchery) culture in ancient times. Tunkou is carved with white poplar and willow as the main raw materials, and then polished smooth with sand, and finally coated with oil paint.

安迪村傣族跳脚舞

　　傣族跳脚舞历史悠久，是治丧时的一种葬仪。每当有老人逝世，主、客家组织人员围着遗体跳脚，以示对死者的敬献和超度。每组跳脚者为一班，由 4 人或多人组成，每人手中各执一串铜铃和一块白毛巾，口中念念有词，围着灵柩按一定旋律边唱边跳，祭奠死者。

**Tiaojiao Dance of the Dai Nationality in Andi Village**
This dance belongs to a kind of ritual funeral rites, which enjoys a long history. Whenever an old man died, his/her families would arrange people to dance Tiaojiao (hop) around the remains to show their respect to and release the soul of the dead person and release the soul thereof.

### 龙场猫耳斗

猫耳斗是一种抽烟的烟具,因其斗部状如猫耳而得名。由龙场镇铜匠李应拔五兄弟所创,至今已传承五代。猫耳斗由红木烟杆和铜饰品两部分组成。木料部分经挖斗、搂空、刨光、雕饰、上油后制成烟杆;铜部件根据需要先将铜片切成坯条进行锻打、焊接,然后镂槽嵌丝、熔铸錾花、花草等图案;最后在烟杆的前端和斗部分别包上加工雕饰好的铜皮饰品。

### Maoer Dou in Longchang County

It is a set for smoking, and named so because the pipe part is cat ear-shaped. This smoke pan was created by coppersmith Li Yingba with his four brothers in Longchang County and has been passed down to the fifth generation till now. It is constituted by two parts: redwood tobacco stem and copper ornament.

### 宣威火腿

宣威火腿因产于宣威市而得名，是宣威汉族在数百年腌腊肉的实践中创造出的腊肉精品，云南著名特产之一，与浙江金华火腿齐名。其形状似琵琶，瘦肉呈鲜红色，肥肉呈乳白色，富含多种营养物质。

### Xuanwei Ham

Xuanwei ham was named so because of its origin of place. It registers a role model of preserved meat, which was created by the Han people in Xuanwei based on hundreds of years' practice in making preserved meat. The ham is pipa-shaped (pipa is a Chinese instrument) and its lean part is bright red and the fat part milk white.

倘塘黄豆腐

倘塘镇由汉、回、彝、苗等多民族杂居而成，明洪武年间（1368年～1398年），伴随着汉族的迁徙，带来了制豆腐的技术，最后演变为倘塘黄豆腐。其做法是把白豆腐用小块的纱布包裹起来，浸放在姜黄汤中煮，黄色的汁水渗入到豆腐块的外层后就变成了黄豆腐。

### Bean Curd of Tangtang Town

Tangtang Town is home to people from different ethnic groups, including the Han, the Hui, the Yi and the Miao. During the reign of the Emperor Hongwu (Zhu Yuanzhang) of the Ming Dynasty (1368–1398), the Han people brought here the technology of making tofu, thus creating the locally special bean curd.

# 昭通市
Zhaotong City

> 大山包

　　位于昭通市昭阳区，距城区 79 千米。大山包地处滇东北五莲峰山脉，海拔 3100～3140 米，年平均气温 6.2℃，由鸡公山大峡谷和大海子两个主要景区组成。该处也是国家一级保护动物黑颈鹤的栖息地。

### Dashanbao

It is located in Zhaoyang District, Zhaotong City, and 79 kilometers away from the urban district. Dashanbao sits in the Wulianfeng Mountain which is in the northeast of Yunnan. At an elevation ranging from 3100 meters to 3140 meters, Dashanbao is consisted of two scenic areas: Jigongshan Great Valley and Dahaizi.

### 大药山

位于昭通市巧家县境内。大药山是乌蒙山群体的一座名山，是当地人心中的圣山。山体面积 220 平方千米，主峰轿顶山海拔 4041.6 米，为滇东北第一高峰。大药山下居住着汉、彝、苗、回、布依等多个民族。

## Dayao Mountain

Located in Qiaojia County, Zhaotong City, Dayao Mountain is a well-known mountain in the group of Wu-meng Mountain, with a mountain area of 220 square kilometers. Its main peak (Jiaoding Mountain) stands at an elevation of 4041.6 meters, marking the highest peak in northeast Yunnan.

### 赖石山

位于昭通市巧家县崇溪乡西北侧。赖石山海拔3303米,是崇溪的最高峰,因山顶石峰林立得名赖石山。赖石山上的石峰形态万千,或矗立或斜靠,造型独特,均为自然形成。

### Laishi Mountain

Located in the northwestern side of Chongxi Township, Qiaojia County, Zhaotong City, it stands at the altitude of 3,303 meters, representing the highest peak in Chongxi Township. Laishi Mountain is named so because of clusters of stone peaks on its peak.

### 黄连河瀑布

位于昭通市大关县。面积25平方千米,内有大小瀑布47条,最大瀑布落差可达147米。景区分为黄连河片区、上高桥片区和罗汉坝片区,有团圆瀑、水帘长廊、白象洞等景观。

### Huanglianhe Waterfall

It is located in Daguan County, covering an area of 25 square kilometers. It is home to 47 waterfalls, among which the fall of the largest one reaches 147 meters. There are many scenic spots in the area, such as Re-union Fall, Water Curtain Corridor and Baixiang (White Elephant) Cave.

### 大雪山原始森林

　　位于昭通市威信县、彝良县及四川珙县、筠连县4县交界处，因积雪早融雪迟，得名大雪山。海拔1600米，曾是红军川滇黔游击纵队主要活动基地。林区面积21.53平方千米，原始生态保持较好。

### Primitive Forest in Snow Mountain

It is located in the intersection of 4 counties (Weixin County and Yiliang County in Zhaotong City, and Gong County and Junlian County in Sichuan Province), standing at the altitude of 1,600 meters. Snow Mountain is named so because snows here accumulate earlier but melt later. The forest covers an area of 21.53 square kilometers and maintains well the primitive ecology.

### 天台山溶洞

位于昭通市威信县麟凤乡。天台山溶洞被称为"西南第一洞",形成于2.3亿~2.8亿年前。溶洞共4层,每层高度20~50米,洞与洞互相贯通。洞内有石径、石廊、石梯、石桥、石洞等景观。

### The Karst Cave of Tiantai Mountain

Located in Linfeng Township, Weixin County, Zhaotong City, this karst cave took shape about 230 million to 280 million years ago and is reputed as "the first cave in Southwest China". There are 4 layers in this cave, each at a height of 20 to 50 meters, and the caves therein are connected with each other.

### 豆沙关

位于昭通市盐津县西南22千米处五尺道的咽喉位置。五尺道始建于秦，是古时四川通向云南的重要通道。豆沙关古称石门关，始建于隋，是通往古南滇的第一关，其城门上刻有"石门关"三字。

### Doushaguan Pass

It is located in checkpoint of the Wuchi (five chi, 1 chi equals to about 1.1 feet) Road, and 22 kilometers in the southwest of Yanjin County, Zhaotong City. Wuchi Road was established in the Qin Dynasty (221–207B.C.), serving as an important pass connecting Sichuan and Yunnan in ancient times. Doushaguan Pass was firstly built in the Sui Dynasty (581–619A.D.) and named Shimenguan Pass in ancient times.

| 昭通古城 |

位于昭通市昭阳区。始建于清雍正九年（1731年）；20世纪30年代中叶，昭通古城内已有大小街道64条；现仍较好地保存有昭通传统市井文化和街巷风貌。古城有四门，东为抚镇门，南为敉宁门，西为济川门，北为趣马门。图为抚镇门。

## Zhaotong Ancient City

Located in Zhaoyang District, Zhaotong City, it was first established in 1731 (the 9th year during the reign of Emperor Yongzheng in the Qing Dynasty). The ancient city has four gates: the eastern one is called Fuzhen Gate, the southern one Mining Gate, the western one Jichuan Gate and the northern one Quma Gate. Fuzhen Gate is shown in the picture.

昭通古城·过街楼

位于昭通市昭阳区昭通古城内。过街楼是昭通古城的商业中心，商铺从过街楼向四周扩散而建。

## Zhaotong Ancient City · Street-across Building

It is located in the Zhaotong Ancient City, Zhaoyang District, Zhaotong City, serving as a commercial center of the Zhaotong Ancient City.

**昭通古城·昭通镇署衙门**

位于昭通市昭阳区昭通古城中心。署衙门是古时昭通古城的行政机构，是中国封建社会政权衙门的实物标本和历史见证，十分珍贵。

### Zhaotong Ancient City · Yamen (government office) of Zhaotong Town

Shuyamen is located in the center of the Zhaotong Ancient City in Zhaoyang District, Zhaotong City. It served as the administrative institution of the Zhaotong Ancient City in ancient times, the physical specimen and historical witness of Yamen in the regime of China's feudal society.

昭通古城·八角亭

　　位于昭通市昭阳区昭通古城。始建于清道光十三年(1892年)，1952年拆毁，1988年重建。八角亭屋脊以八龙为饰，是昭通城古典建筑的代表之作。

**Zhaotong Ancient City · Bajiao (Octagonal) Pavilion**

Located in Zhaotong Ancient City, Zhaoyang District, Zhaotong City, it was built in 1892 (the 13th year during the reign of the Emperor Daoguang in the Qing Dynasty), demolished in 1952 and rebuilt in 1988. Bajiao (Octagonal) Pavilion serves as a masterpiece of classical architecture in Zhaotong Ancient City.

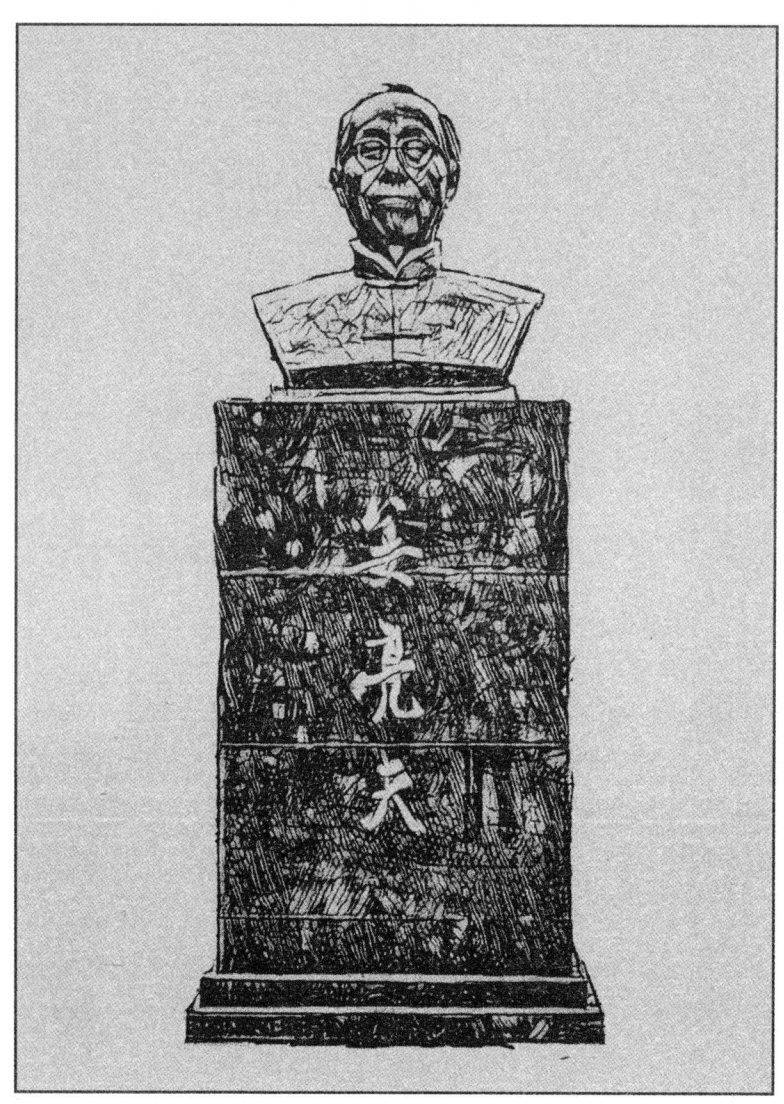

### 昭通古城·姜亮夫雕像

位于昭通市昭阳区昭通古城姜亮夫故居内。姜亮夫（1902年～1995年），云南昭通人，著名的楚辞学、敦煌学、语言音韵学、历史文献学家、教育家。

### Zhaotong Ancient City · Jiang Liangfu Sculpture

It is located in the Jiang Liangfu Former Residence of Zhaotong Ancient City, Zhaoyang District, Zhaotong City. Jiang Liangfu (1902-1995), a native of Zhaotong in Yunnan, is a renowned expert on the study of the Songs of Chu and educationalist.

昭通古城·辕门口钟楼

位于昭通市昭阳区北正街辕门口广场，建成于2009年。钟楼为古城恢复建设中增添的一处仿古建筑，共4层，高14.7米，占地面积900平方米。顶层悬挂有大钟，敲钟时，数里外皆可听到。

## Zhaotong Ancient City · Yuanmenkou Bell Tower

Located at the Yuanmenkou Square of Beizheng Street in Zhaoyang District, Zhaotong City, it was completed in 2009. This four-story tower, at a height of 14.7 meters, is a pseudo-classic newly-built architecture in the project of restoring the ancient city.

### 大龙洞道观

位于昭通市昭阳区北闸镇九龙山上。建于清乾隆年间（1736年~1796年），1982年设立为道教活动场所。建筑面积1002.4平方米，道观内有一龙潭，由于泉水的出口形似一个巨大的龙头，故被称为大龙洞。

### Taoist Temple in Dalong Cave

Located in Jiulong Mountain of Beizha Town, Zhaoyang District, Zhaotong City, it was established during the reign of Emperor Qianlong in the Qing Dynasty (1736–1796), and was set up as a place in 1982 for holding Taoist-related activities. This temple covers a floor area of 1,002.4 square kilometers.

### 清官亭

位于昭通市昭阳区西北隅。原名三多塘，始建于清嘉庆十三年（1808年），是当时县令王禹甸为解决饮水问题带头捐资修建的。王禹为官清廉，故后人改名清官亭。亭为二层回廊水榭，前面有石桥相通，建筑面积305平方米。

### Qingguan (Honest and Upright Official) Pavilion

Located in the northwestern corner of Zhaoyang District, Zhaotong City, it was built in 1808 (the 13th year during the reign of Emperor Jiaqing in the Qing Dynasty), funded by the money raised by the county magistrate Wang Yudian at that time in order to facilitate the supplies of drinkable water. This two-story pavilion covers an area of 305 square meters and is connected with the stone bridge forward.

元宝山公园

　　位于昭通市昭阳区东南元宝山脚下，为著名的"昭阳八景"之一，因景色宜人，有"宝山环翠"之说。整个公园占地面积8670平方米，建筑面积为820平方米，有重檐四方亭、重檐八角亭、回廊、鱼池、花园等景观。

## Yuanbaoshan Park

Yuanbaoshan Park is located in the foot of Yuanbao (shoe-shaped gold ingot) Mountain, in the southeast of Zhaoyang District, Zhaotong City. It is among the well-known "Eight Great Sights of Zhaoyang", covering an area of 8,670 square meters and boasting scenery such as double-eave square pavilions, winding corridors, fishponds and gardens.

[望海公园]

位于昭通市昭阳区凤凰山麓。2010年望海公园正式建成,为人工水体公园。有恩波楼、人工湖、人造沙滩、人造岛等景点。

## Wanghai (sea-viewing) Park

Located in the foot of Phoenix Mountain, Zhaoyang District, Zhaotong City, Wanghai Park was officially completed in 2010. It is an artificial water park, boasting scenic spots such as Enbo Tower, artificial lake and artificial beach.

### 望海公园·恩波楼

位于昭通市昭阳区望海公园内。又名望海楼，始建于清乾隆二十五年（1760年），咸丰年间（1851年～1861年）毁于大火，光绪末年杨履恒募巨资重建，并在楼前增设屋宅、回廊、亭子、花木等景观。

### Wanghai Park · Enbo Tower

Located in Wanghai Park in Zhaoyang District, Zhaotong City, Enbo Tower, also named Wanghai Tower, was built in 1760 (the 25$^{th}$ year during the reign of Emperor Qianlong in the Qing Dynasty). During the reign of Emperor Xianfeng, the tower was ruined in a great fire and was then reconstructed during the late years of Emperor Guangxu's reign.

望海公园·望海阁

位于昭通市昭阳区望海公园石桥南边的一座小岛上。图为望海阁掩映在葱郁的树木间。

## Wanghai Park · Wanghai Pavilion

Located in an island in the south of Wanghai Park's stone bridge, Zhaoyang District, Zhaotong City, this pavilion is half-hidden among luxuriant trees.

### 老孔雀雕塑

　　位于昭通市昭阳区。始建于1991年，由于雕塑面朝凤凰山方向，故俗称为"老孔雀"。雕塑高16米左右，为一只站立的凤凰，下面环岛周围有工、农、商、学、兵的人物造型雕塑。该雕塑曾是昭通的地标性建筑。2015年被拆除。

### Old Peacock Sculpture

Located in Zhaoyang District, Zhaotong City, it was established in 1991. It is about 16 meters high as a standing phoenix. It was once a landmark building for Zhaotong but was torn down in 2015.

{罗炳辉将军像}

位于昭通市昭阳区北顺城街罗炳辉广场。罗炳辉（1897年~1946年），昭通市彝良县人，是新中国成立后中央军委认定的解放军36个军事家之一。塑像为铜铸，高3.5米，基座高1.8米，总高5.3米。

## Sculpture of General Luo Binghui

It is located at Luo Binghui Square in Beishuncheng Street, Zhaoyang District, Zhaotong City. Luo Binghui (1897-1947), a native of Yiliang County, Zhaotong City, is among the 36 strategists of the People's Liberation Army entitled by China's Central Military Commission (CMC) after the founding of People's Republic of China. The sculpture is cast in bronze, standing at 3.5 meters and the total height is 5.3 meters high (its base is 1.8 meters high).

### 昭通市博物馆

　　位于昭通市昭阳区朱提大道旁，建成于2011年。博物馆外观为一艘气势恢宏的大船和一方古朴的汉印，取承载历史、开拓进取之寓意。占地面积3722平方米，展区面积6500平方米，内藏有文物1.6万余件。

### Zhaotong Museum

Located beside Zhuti Avenue in Zhaoyang District, Zhaotong City, this museum was completed in 2011, covering an area of 3,722 square meters and the exhibition area is 6,500 square meters. There are more than 16,000 copies of cultural relics in the museum's collection.

孟孝琚碑

　　位于昭通市昭阳区第三中学内。孟孝琚碑出土于清光绪二十七年（1901年），据考证为东汉永寿三年（157年）所立。上端断残，下端完整，左有龙纹，右有虎纹，下有龟纹。残碑高1.33米，宽0.96米，碑文为隶书，共15行，存256字。

**Meng Xiaoju Stele**
Located in No.3 Senior High School in Zhaoyang District, Zhaotong City, this stele was unearthed in 1901 (the 27th year during the reign of Emperor Guangxu in the Qing Dynasty). It is reported to be built in 157 (the 3rd during the reign of Emperor Yongshou in the East Han Dynasty). It is 1.33 meters high, 0.96 meters wide with 15 lines of 256 Lishu characters (official script at that time) in total.

【拖姑清真寺·正殿】

位于昭通市鲁甸县城东约10千米的桃源回族乡拖姑村,始建于清雍正八年(1730年)。全寺由正殿、唤醒楼、无倦堂、后亭、厢房、水房、照壁等组成,共有殿阁楼亭30余间,是云南省五大古寺之一。

**Tuogu Mosque · Main Hall**
Located in Tuogu Village of the Hui Autonomous Township in Taoyuan, 10 kilometers in the east of Ludian County's downtown, Zhaotong City, it was first built in 1730 (the 8th year during the reign of Emperor Yongzheng in the Qing Dynasty). The mosque, reputed as one of the five temples in Yunnan Province, boasts over 30 palaces, pavilions, halls and towers.

{ 拖姑清真寺·唤醒楼 }

　　位于昭通市鲁甸县桃源回族乡拖姑村拖姑清真寺内。唤醒楼是伊斯兰教寺院中特有的建筑,为阿訇观月、斋戒之用。

Tuogu Mosque · Wakening Tower

Located in Tuogu Mosque in Ludian County, Zhaotong City, the Wakening Tower serves as a unique building in Islamic mosques and is used for fasting and for the imam (a person who presides over the religious affairs of a mosque) to watch the moon.

> 崇文阁

　　位于昭通市鲁甸县。建于清乾隆四十二年（1777年）。崇文阁是供奉儒家先贤的圣地，原阁已毁，尚留五株古杉傲然屹立。重建于2005年，由台阶、牌坊、泮池、孺园、砚池斋、墨客轩、先师殿、九曲回廊等部分组成。

### Chongwen Pavilion

Located in Ludian County, Zhaotong City, it was established in 1777 (the 42$^{nd}$ year during the reign of Emperor Qianlong in the Qing Dynasty). As a sacred place to pay tribute to Confucianism sages, the original Chongwen Pavilion had been destroyed and the new one was reconstructed in 2005.

安氏土司墓

　　位于昭通市永善县桧溪镇政府驻地。安氏土司墓有三冢，占地面积4000平方米，是中国西南边陲土司文化的实物见证。其中安永长土司墓建于清朝道光三年（1823年），保存完好。墓高5.1米，宽8.8米，墓碑上刻有各种精细的图案。

## Chieftain Cemetery of the An

Located in the government resident of Guixi Town, Yongshan County, Zhaotong City, Chieftain Cemetery of the An has three tombs, among which the well-preserved An Yongchang Chieftain Cemetery was built in 1823 (the 3rd year during the reign of Emperor Daoguang in the Qing Dynasty). This cemetery is 5.1 meters high and 8.8 meters wide with varieties of delicate patterns carved on it.

### 曾泽生将军故居

位于昭通市永善县大兴镇大兴村驿马沟。曾泽生（1902年～1973年）永善大兴人，毕业于黄埔军校，曾任滇军、国民党军将领，参加过台儿庄战役和武汉、长沙等战役。故居为传统土木结构四合院，由大门、正厅、右厢房、左厢房、下天房、炮楼、碉楼、厨房等部分组成。

### General Zeng Zesheng's Former Residence

It is located in Yimagou in Daxing Village, Daxing Town, Yongshan County, Zhaotong City. Zeng Zesheng (1902–1973), a native of Daxing Village in Yongshan County, was graduated from the Huangpu Military Academy. He had engaged in several battles such as the battle of Tai'erzhuang and the battles defending Wuhan and Changsha. This residence is a quadrangle dwelling with traditional civil structure.

> 牛街古镇

　　位于昭通市彝良县东北部川滇边界处。始建于东汉时期,已有 1000 多年的历史。古镇至今仍保留有明清时期街道两条、木竹质结构民居 400 多间。牛街古镇交通便利,是彝良的"北大门",自古以来就商贾云集、商业繁荣,被称为"小香港"。

## Niujie Ancient Town

It is located in the border of Sichuan-Yunnan, the northeast of Yiliang County, Zhaotong City. First built in the Eastern Han Dynasty (25-220), this ancient town enjoys a history of over 1,000 years. With convenient transportation, numerous merchants and prosperous business, the ancient town is reputed as "little Hong Kong".

罗炳辉将军故居

位于昭通市彝良县角奎镇阿都办事处偏坡寨。为1987年在原址按原貌重建。故居坐北向南，为土木结构草房3间。是罗炳辉将军17岁从军前的旧居，陈列有将军当时使用的生活用具。

## General Luo Binghui's Former Residence

Located in Pianpo Village, Adu Township, Jiaokui Town, Yiliang County, Zhaotong City, it was rebuilt in 1987 in the former site according to its original appearance. This former residence, facing south, is a complex including 3 thatched cottages, which was lived by General Luo Binghui before he joined the army when he was 17 years old.

夫人坝

  位于昭通市绥江县城东 20 千米处，三面临崖，一面环山，风景秀丽。夫人坝平均海拔 1280 米，因别具风格的古建筑、山花烂漫的乡景和耐人寻味的传说而得名。

## Furen (lady) Dam

It is located in the place 20 kilometers at the east of urban area of Suijiang County, Zhaotong City. Standing at an average altitude of 1,280 meters, the Furen Dam is named so because it boasts unique ancient-style buildings, flowery countryside scenery and intriguing legends.

### 扎西会议纪念馆

位于昭通市威信县扎西镇东北角。建于 1977 年，是为纪念 1935 年 2 月中共中央政治局在扎西镇等地召开的会议而建立的。陈列馆倚山而建，有上下两层 4 个展室，展厅面积 2590 平方米。共展出图片 170 多幅、红军遗物 70 多件。

### Memorial Hall of Zhaxi Meeting

Located in the northeast corner of Zhaxi Town in Weixin County, Zhaotong City, it was established in 1977 in memory of the meetings held in Zhaxi Towns and other places by the Political Bureau of the Central Committee of the Communist Party of China in February 1935. This two-story hall has four exhibition halls which cover an area of 2,590 square meters.

## 扎西红军烈士陵园

位于昭通市威信县扎西镇。始建于1984年，占地面积4.6万平方米。陵园内建有高10米、碑体边长2米的红军烈士纪念碑一座，其南北两面分别刻有毛泽东书体的"红军烈士纪念碑"和"英勇奋斗的红军万岁"碑文，从东、南、西、北四面台阶皆可步上纪念碑台座。

### Red Army Martyr Cemetery in Zhaxi Town

Located in Zhaxi Town in Weixin County, Zhaotong City and first established in 1984, it covers an area of 46,000 square meters. There stands a Red Army martyr monument with a height of 10 meters and a side length of 2 meters in the cemetery.

水富港

位于昭通市金沙江畔水富县。始建于1974年，位于滇川两省交界处、金沙江末端和长江上游。水富港是云南的第一内陆大港，也是万里长江第一大港。

## Shuifu Port

Located in Shuifu County at the bank of Jinshang River, Zhaotong City, it was first established in 1974. Shuifu Port serves as the largest inland port in Yunnan and the largest port connecting the Yangtze River.

向家坝水电站

位于昭通市水富县与四川省宜宾县交界的金沙江下游河段上，距水富县1500米。2006年正式开工建设，由三峡集团修建。向家坝水电站是金沙江水电基地最后一级水电站，以发电为主，同时兼有改善通航条件、防洪、灌溉、拦沙等作用。

## Xiangjiaba Hydropower Station

It is located in the lower reach of Jinsha River where Yibin County (in Sichuan Province) and Shuifu County (in Zhaotong City) meets. 1,500 meters from Shuifu County, this station was firstly established in 2006. The Xiangjiaba Hydropower Station is mainly set for power generation coupled with functions such as navigation improvement, flood control, irrigation and sand-resistance.

### 昭通端公戏

昭通端公戏是云南民间戏曲剧种之一，流行于昭通市镇雄、彝良、大关、盐津、巧家、永善、威信、绥江、昭阳等地，主要在庆菩萨、庆坛、打傩、阳戏及斋醮等仪式活动中演出，因由端公表演而名。端公戏于明清时期由江西、四川等地传入，分为正戏和耍戏两种。

### Duangong Opera in Zhaotong

As one of the folk operas in Yunnan, it is mainly performed in ceremonial activities, enjoying popularity in places such as Yiliang County and Zhaoyang County in Zhaotong City. This opera, classified into Zhengxi and Shuaxi, was introduced to Yunnan from Jiangxi and Sichuan during the Ming and the Qing Dynasties.

### 昭通端公戏·面具

端公戏中所戴面具,多为狰狞面目,代表着妖魔鬼怪。面具多为木制,以丁木、梨木、杨木为料,经雕镌镂刻、涂敷色彩而成。造型夸张、怪诞,具有原始、古拙的特色。

**Duangong Opera in Zhaotong · Mask**

Masks worn in the Duangong Opera are mostly fiendish and ferocious as they represent demons and ghosts. These masks are mainly made of wood, with exaggerated and weird expressions.

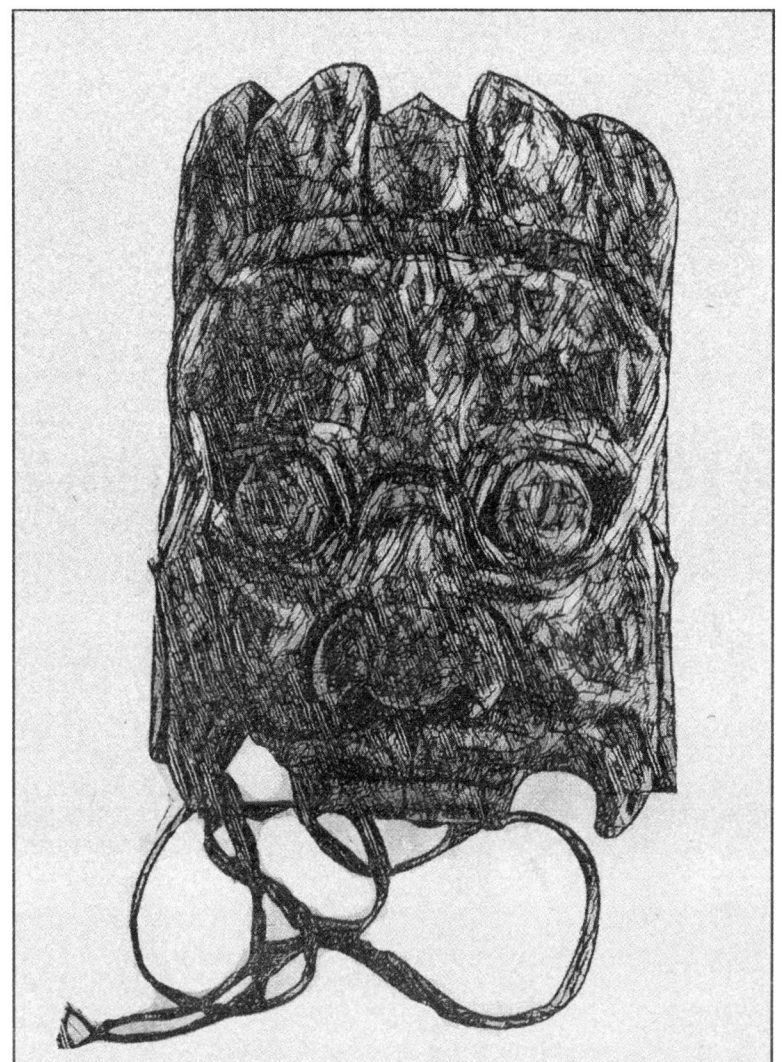

四筒鼓舞

　　四筒鼓舞是流传于昭通市的传统祭祀舞蹈。又称跳鼓、跳丧鼓，距今已有3000多年历史，是由男性集体演跳的丧葬舞蹈。因舞者四人身挎筒鼓击之、舞之而得名。为昭通民间较有特色和影响的舞蹈之一。

## Si-tong Drum Dance

Si-tong drum dance serves as a traditional sacrificial dance circulated in Zhaotong City, enjoying a history of 3,000 years. It is a kind of funeral dance performed by a group of men.

四筒鼓舞 · 四筒鼓

  在四筒鼓舞中，虽有其他乐器转鼓、红绫、锣、钹、铙、镲、铛的参与，但四筒鼓始终处于核心位置。据《昭通志稿》描述："四筒鼓，形长，削木为之，两头蒙以皮，多丧礼用之，以为跳舞。"

### Si-tong Drum Dance · Si-tong Drum

In four-bronze-drum dance, despite the involvement of other instruments such as gongs, cymbals (Nao and Bo), the wood-made four bronze drum remains the core one.

### 小寨樱桃

　　小寨樱桃是昭通市鲁甸县小寨乡的特产，种植历史已有300多年。小寨樱桃花白色带红晕，果实近于珠形，鲜红水灵，肉厚核小，甜味浓郁。

### Xiaozhai Cherry

Xiaozhai cherry is a specialty of Xiaozhai Township in Ludian County, Zhaotong City, enjoying a cultivation history of over 300 years. Xiaozhai cherry boasts thick pulp, small pit and tastes very sweet.

> 回族刺绣

鲁甸回族刺绣历史悠久，图案精美，色泽亮丽，显现了滇东北回族崇尚自然、追求素雅的偏好，具有较高的艺术价值。

### Embroidery of the Hui Nationality

It enjoys a long and profound history, demonstrating that the Hui people in northeast Yunnan are in the worship of the nature and in pursuit of simplicity and elegance. The embroidery is of high artistic values.

梭山竹编

梭山竹编是昭通市鲁甸县梭山乡的特产，历史悠久，为梭山地区传统手工艺品，有很高的艺术和实用价值。成品有簸箕、笓、篮、蒸笼、筲箕、背箩、箩筐等。

## Suoshan Bamboo Weaving

Suoshan bamboo weaving is a specialty of Suoshan Township in Ludian County, Zhaotong City, enjoying a long history. Its finished products include dustpans, steamers, back baskets and other kinds of baskets.

炉房斑铜制作

斑铜工艺是云南特有的传统工艺。巧家县炉房乡噜布村斑铜制作主要以打制壶、锅、盆、碗等生活实用器具为主,传承了"堂琅铜洗"的一些工艺技法,其铜具造型不加过多的装饰,外形饱满、浑厚,具有汉代器物造型的审美特征。

**Variegated Copperware Manufacturing in Lufang Township**
The manufacturing of variegated copperware is a unique traditional technology in Yunnan. The variegated copperware in Lubu Village, Lufang Township, Qiaojia County is mainly made into practical tools for life. The copper tools are free from excessive decorations but with full and vigorous shape.

小碗红糖

俗称碗碗糖，产于昭通市巧家县金沙江沿岸地区，以甘蔗为原料用土法熬制而成。其工序有压榨、加热、制糖、包扎等，制成的红糖呈红黄色，香气浓郁，品味纯正。

## Brown Sugar Contained by Small Bowl

Commonly named as Wanwan Sugar, it is produced in the coastal area of Jinsha River in Qiaojia County, Zhaotong City. The sugar is made according to local decoction method with sugar canes as the raw materials. The already made brown sugar is presented to be reddish yellow with rich fragrance.

僰人悬棺

僰人悬棺是古代葬式的一种。人死后，亲属殓遗体入棺，将木棺置于崖洞中、崖缝内或半悬于崖外。所选崖洞往往陡峭高危、无从攀登，悬置越高，越是表示对死者的尊敬。

## Boren Suspending Coffin

It is an ancient funeral ceremony. After the death of someone, his or her families put the body into coffin and then the coffin is placed into the cliff cave. The selected cave is usually in dangerously precipitous position. The higher the cave is placed, the more respect is shown to the deceased.

**马楠苗族芦笙舞**

苗族芦笙舞历史悠久，起源于祭祀活动。跳芦笙舞时，男子吹奏芦笙，女子伴舞，舞姿优美，节奏明快。马楠乡的芦笙舞为永善县芦笙舞的代表，以传承正统、艺术性强、水准较高而闻名。

**Lusheng Dance of the Miao Nationality in Ma'nan**

It is originated from sacrificial activities, enjoying a long history. In Lusheng dance, men are responsible for playing Lusheng and women for dancing. The Lusheng dance in Ma'nan Township is the representative of those in Yongshan County.

### 伍寨乡彝族月琴

彝族月琴，彝语称"弦子"，是彝族人常用的弹弦乐器。伍寨乡为月琴之乡。月琴用上好楠木制成，其顶端雕有含珠龙头，龙头下左右各布有两只木刻的调弦在琴腰上，可以调节琴弦的松紧。根据不同音调的需要，琴弦分为多段，在不同段上可分别弹出由底到高的各种音调。

### Yueqin of the Yi Nationality in Wuzhai Township

It is a commonly used string instrument of the Yi people. Yueqin is a four-stringed plucked instrument with a full-moon-shaped sound box, and made of superior proebe bournei, on the top of which craved a dragon's head with a pearl in its mouth. Under the head, there are two woodcut tuners on the waist of the instrument, which can adjust the tightness of the strings.

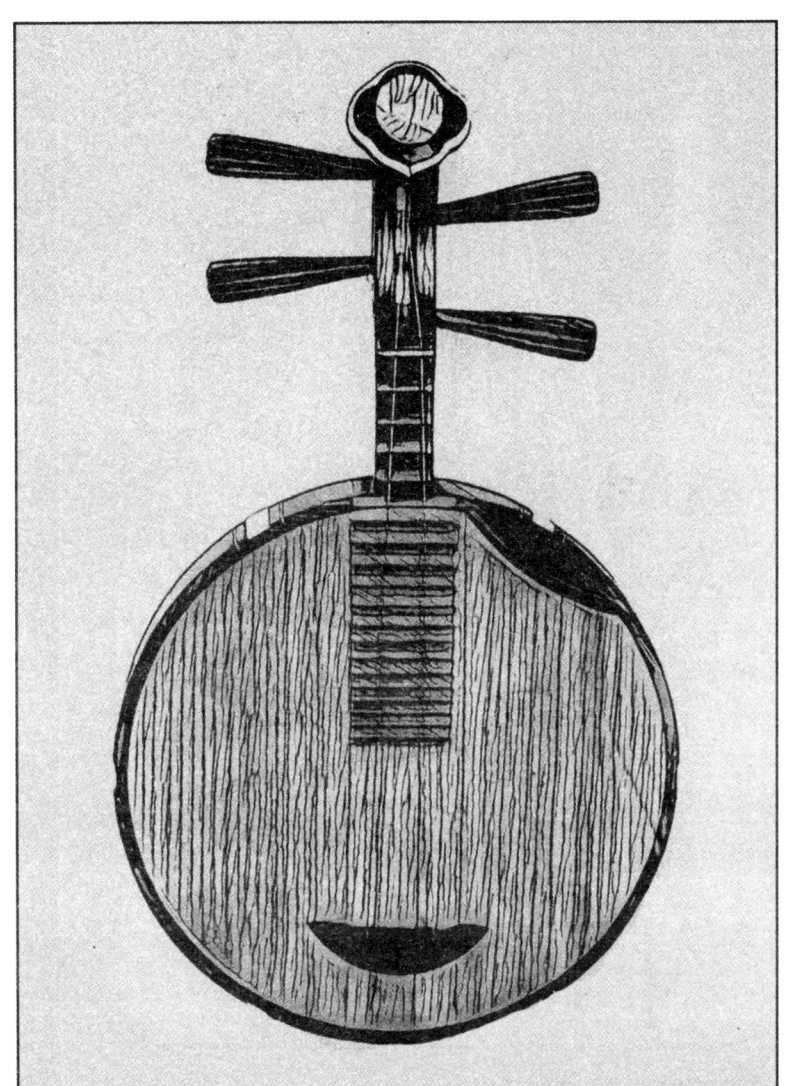

{ 手工皮棉纸 }

　　昭通市彝良县至今仍然保留着用树皮造纸的传统技艺，具有选材精、做工细、工艺严谨的特色。制成的皮棉纸的厚度约为书写纸的 2～3 倍，韧性强，不易破裂，经久耐用。

## Handmade Lint Paper

Yiliang County in Zhaotong City maintains the traditional crafts of making paper with barks. The already made lint paper with strong resilience is enduring and hard to be fractured.

> 芦笙制作

　　芦笙是苗族的传统乐器,由笙斗、笙管、簧片和共鸣管组成。昭通市威信县芦笙制作有悠久的历史,其制作工序繁杂,有选料、烤料、打制簧片、制作竹木部件、装簧片、定音等几十道工序。

## Lusheng Manufacturing

Lusheng, a traditional instrument of the Miao Nationality, is constituted of its body, pipe, reed and resonance tube. Weixin County in Zhaotong City boasts a profound history of manufacturing Lusheng.